AF302579

CALCULATING YOUR ENNEAGRAM

Discover your true self

Written by Valérie Debruche
Translated by Emma Hanna

Coaching | 50MINUTES.com

50MINUTES.com

PROPEL
YOUR BUSINESS FORWARD!

NETWORKING
Venture outside your close circle
and connect with other professionals

Effective CV Writing

Resolving Office Conflict

Boost Your Concentration

Find Your Work-Life Balance

www.50minutes.com

THE ENNEAGRAM OF PERSONALITY

- **Problem:** what is the Enneagram and how can it help us as we strive towards personal fulfilment?
- **Uses:** this self-analysis technique facilitates targeted personal development in order to help us find a path that suits us, particularly in a professional context.
- **Professional context:** human resources, work psychology, communication, management.
- **FAQs:**
  - Surely using the Enneagram to analyse people's personalities is really about putting people in boxes?
  - Will examining my personality through the lens of Enneagram theory really help me to understand myself more fully?
  - How can I apply Enneagram theory in my professional life?
  - Is there an ideal profession for each type?
  - Are there some types which are fundamen-

tally incapable of understanding each other?
  ◦ Can my type change over time?

Finding your path, carving out a place for yourself and flourishing at work are some of the challenges that anyone who works is sure to come up against. Everyone's success in these matters hinges on how well they know themselves, but this can often seem like an insurmountable challenge in and of itself. This is where a tool such as the Enneagram can come in very useful.

The Enneagram is a method of analysing your own personality, which will then help you to focus your professional efforts more effectively and obtain better results. It focuses on an individual's strengths and weaknesses, as well as the ways of bringing out the best in them. It can also give you some idea of the answers to questions such as: "How can I find a path to success that will be fulfilling for me?" and "How can I unlock the full potential of my personality?"

At one point or another, almost all of us will feel at least a flicker of doubt over how wisely we chose our career path. Similarly, it is far from unusual to feel as though you are struggling to gain any ground in your personal and professional development. The Enneagram offers you a way of carrying out self-analysis which will help you to control your own behaviour.

Although it is simple to apply, certain aspects of the Enneagram method can seem complex, as it is not simply a way of sorting personality types into boxes: it also offers solutions.

ENNEAGRAM INSIGHTS: THE BASICS

WHAT IS THE ENNEAGRAM?

The Enneagram is a psychological theory which dates back to Antiquity, and has been reinterpreted by the Christian and Sufi communities, among others, in the intervening years. Until recently, the Enneagram was always viewed in a religious or philosophical context, but in the 1970s it re-emerged in the field of psychology in the United States, and since then the technique has become commonplace in the professional sector. Its newly restored popularity can primarily be attributed to the Chilean psychiatrist Claudio Naranjo (born in 1932), who studied the topic in depth for many years and developed the definitions of the nine personality types which make up the Enneagram. In the intervening decades, the use of the Enneagram also became widespread in the spiritual, business and education sectors, and proved equally effective in these fields. Experts have identified three major advantages of this revised method, among others:

- it is a totally individualised method of analysis;
- it takes the triune brain model into account, which allows it to focus more on a person's motivations than their behaviour;
- it is dynamic, as each analysis provides solutions rather than simply categorising the individual.

The triune brain model

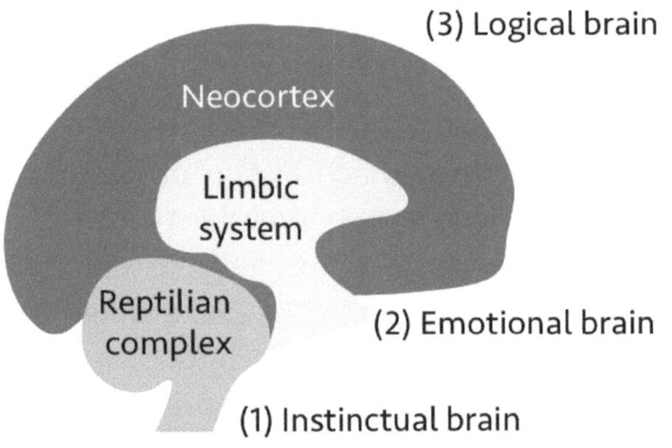

Etymologically speaking, the word "enneagram" denotes a nine-sided geometric figure (from the Greek *ennea*, meaning "nine", and *gramma*, meaning "letter" or "drawing"), reflecting how the purpose of this method is to classify each subject of analysis into one of the nine personality types that Enneagram theory is based on. As such, the enneagram figure takes the form of a circle with nine points, known as "bases", dotted around its circumference. Each of these bases corresponds to a "type", which in the context of personality analysis is defined by several predominant personality traits related to an individual's motivations.

The enneagram

Motivation

1. To avoid imperfection
2. To avoid rejection
3. To avoid failure
4. To avoid ordinariness
5. To avoid worthlessness
6. To avoid insecurity
7. To avoid pain
8. To avoid weakness
9. To avoid conflict

The Enneagram can help individuals to improve both their relationships and their wellbeing in a wide variety of contexts, although it is considered particularly well-suited for use in the world of work. Its effectiveness has proven unparalleled in training programmes and as a guideline during organisational reshuffles. In this field, it is able to reveal an individual's particular talents and to predict when certain weaknesses are likely to surface, all by taking that person's "type" into consideration. The Enneagram is first and foremost a dynamic approach, and provides users with charts which allow them to predict both their own reactions and other people's reactions, and by extension, to find professional positions to which they are better suited. When used correctly and comprehensively, its impact can go far beyond your personal expectations.

The aim of this overview of the Enneagram is to familiarise you with the main concepts that the method involves. Bearing in mind that, depending on how much detail you require, the length of time required to create a full Enneagram profile for an individual can vary a great deal, in this guide we will try to help you pinpoint your type without the use of a questionnaire. Once you have an idea of your type, we will then provide an overview of the characteristics of each one.

Advice for employers

You may be wondering whether or not it is really worth spending valuable working hours on an introduction to the Enneagram. However, problems and misunderstandings can easily arise between employees, or between employees and their employers, sparking tensions in the workplace. This is often down to a lack of understanding about how our motivations and the ways we process information differ from person to person. In fact, sometimes we fail to fully comprehend our own reasons for acting in a certain way. The Enneagram not only gives us the opportunity to get to know ourselves better and to improve our own wellbeing, but also, and most importantly, it gives us insight into the different motivations that drive those around us. Understanding how your colleagues think and react is a crucial first step in forestalling any future conflicts.

THE ENNEAGRAM: THE FREEDOM TO ANALYSE YOURSELF

An individual tool

The Enneagram is a unique tool – although self-help techniques and wellness therapy are becoming more and more widespread in our society, the Enneagram complements them perfectly as a self-prescribed remedy. The specific steps to follow to put the Enneagram into practice are as follows:

- realise that you want to get to know yourself better (an essential part of the process which should not be dismissed out of hand);
- discover your type and locate your personality on the Enneagram;
- discover the solutions offered by the Enneagram and related literature so that you can manage your type as effectively as possible (by eliminating any unhealthy behaviours);
- apply what you have learned from the Enneagram in your daily life and, of course, in the workplace.

Of course, experts play a role in each of these stages, but this in no way diminishes the essence of the process: it always has an individual who wants to make progress in their life at its centre, from the beginning through to the end.

Naranjo has expressed his regret that self-analysis is increasingly undervalued in our society. In fact, psychoanalysts now have a monopoly on personality evaluations and guiding individuals towards improved wellbeing. Naranjo claims, "We cannot afford it at a time when our collective predicament depends much on individual human transformation and when we cannot afford not arousing the potential and motivation of individuals to work on themselves to the extent that they can" (Naranjo, 1994: 269).

The types: a behavioural base

For some people, identifying their dominant type is as simple as glancing through the descriptions of the different Enneagram types. The ease with which you can figure out your type generally depends on how well you know yourself at the start of the process, but this is no guarantee. Self-analysis remains a complex "science" which can be difficult to understand, and you should do as much extra reading on the subject as possible before saying with any certainty that you belong to one type or another – luckily, there is no shortage of related literature.

In this guide, we are going to start by providing you with some definitions which may seem simplistic, but which provide rapid insight into individual personalities without getting bogged down in the details. If you are really struggling to identify with one of the categories provided for each of the aspects of the theory that we have laid out in this guide, take a few days or even a few weeks to reflect on it: pay attention to your own reactions in specific situations, to the way you interact with others, to your goals and priorities, etc. Similarly, do not hesitate to ask your close friends and family for their opinions.

You can also take a test in the form of a questionnaire. In this case, we would advise you to opt for a recognised method, and to take it under the supervision of a qualified psychologist who will be able to help you interpret the results.

At this point, we are trying to define the "base" type, or the dominant type. Of course, an Enneagram type will never be a fully accurate reflection of someone's personality, and one person may identify with various aspects of all of the different types. However, one type ought to be a much more accurate description of your personality than any of the others. This is your dominant type, even though only certain characteristics of that type may apply to you at a given moment.

These dominant types are complemented by "wings". This means that each type is influenced by the types on either side of it, one of which exerts a stronger influence than the other. For example, the dominant wing of a type 9 individual would be either wing 8 or wing 1.

Wings

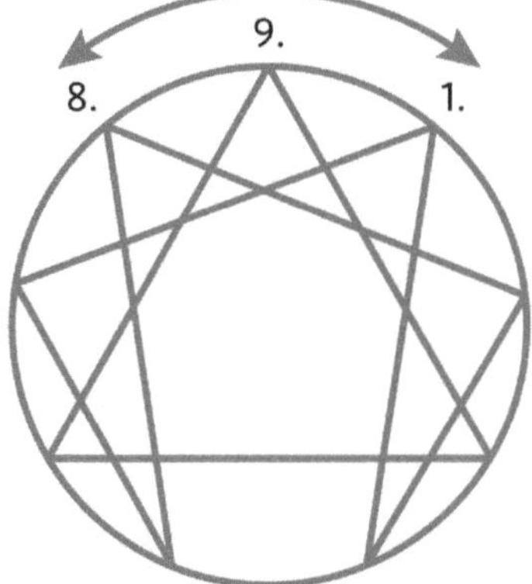

Finally, the Enneagram also includes the directions of integration (growth) and of disintegration (stress) of each type. These are depicted on the enneagram figure by arrows which connect each type to two others, thus indicating the relationships between the types and their behavioural tendencies. The arrow pointing towards each base type indicates its direction of integration, and originates from another type which the individual in question will mimic when they feel fulfilled, safe and content. Conversely, the arrow pointing away from each base type indicates its direction of disintegration, and leads to the type which the individual will imitate when stressed or threatened.

For example, a type 6 who usually feels anxious and suspicious will begin to exhibit the behaviours of a healthy type 9 if their situation changes so that they feel comfortable and begin to thrive; in other words, they will be tolerant and calm. Conversely, a loyal, stable type 6 who is then put under excessive pressure is likely to start acting like an unhealthy type 3 – arrogant and disdainful of others.

Directions of integration and disintegration

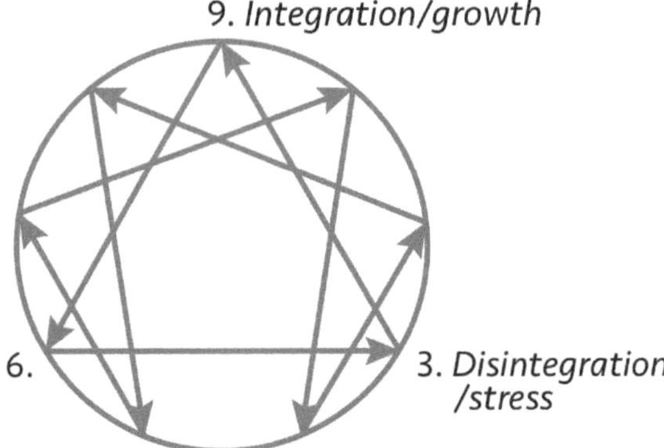

The method

So, how can you identify your type? There are many ways of calculating your Enneagram, the most common of which is a questionnaire. However, this technique can prove time-consuming. Although it is generally supposed to be filled out by the individual in question, one or more close friends or family members can also provide assistance to ensure that your answers are objective. After all, the success of this method hinges on how objectively you are able to view yourself: if you are unable to do so, your assigned type will be incorrect and any resulting efforts towards self-improvement will be ineffective.

In this book, we will guide you through a more intuitive approach to identifying your type (although it is essential to consider it in greater depth if you intend to continue with self-improvement and strengthening your professional relationships). In practice, each of the nine Enneagram types can be placed into sub-categories linked to three different factors:

- your dominant brain;
- your attitude to the world;

- your source of motivation.

In the following section we will summarise the characteristics of each of these sub-categories, which should enable you to hone in on the Enneagram types which correspond most closely to you. Given that this is not a comprehensive approach, it will not necessarily be possible to pinpoint your type using this method alone. Remember, this is just a first step which is intended to help you identify, if not your dominant personality type, at least one of your main personality traits, which you can then use as a base when taking a full test to determine your Enneagram type.

FINDING YOUR TYPE

For each of the three following categories, try to identify the option which best describes your personality as objectively as possible.

Which is your dominant brain?

- **Reptilian brain, "the gut":** you are driven by instinct, are not prone to introspection, make decisions based chiefly on intuition, are mate-

rialistic, and are fond of being in charge.
- **Limbic brain, "the heart":** you are driven by emotions, are prone to self-sacrificing behaviour, yearn for recognition and believe that you receive less than you deserve, and adapt easily to new situations and people.
- **Neocortex, "the head":** you are driven by reason and curiosity, rarely reveal your own thoughts and feelings, never act impulsively, and have self-isolating tendencies.

What is your attitude to the world?

- **Hostile:** you adopt a combative attitude towards others, and feel that the world is against you and you need to impose your own will on it by force.
- **Obliging:** you adopt an accommodating attitude when others ask for help, and feel like you need to conform.
- **Reticent:** you have a self-isolating attitude, and shy away from challenges and assistance alike.

What motivates you?

- **Vanity:** you have limited interest in others and

excessive self-esteem.
- **Conformity:** you are easily swayed by the opinions of others, and obey convention to the detriment of your own needs.
- **Competitiveness:** you are outwardly-focused with a defiant attitude towards others.

The table below summarises this information so that, depending on which of the above categories you relate to most, you should now be able to tentatively identify your Enneagram type.

Type	Dominant brain	Attitude to the world	Motivation
1	Reptilian (gut)	Hostile	Competitiveness
2	Limbic (heart)	Obliging	Vanity
3	Limbic (heart)	Hostile	Conformity
4	Limbic (heart)	Reticent	Competitiveness
5	Neocortex (head)	Reticent	Vanity
6	Neocortex (head)	Obliging	Conformity
7	Neocortex (head)	Obliging	Competitiveness
8	Reptilian (gut)	Hostile	Vanity
9	Reptilian (gut)	Reticent	Conformity

Each type is motivated by different factors than the other types, which is the reason for many disagreements and misunderstandings, particularly in the workplace. Applying Enneagram theory to understand what drives us personally and to decipher our colleagues' motivations allows for a better understanding of individual reactions. This leaves us better prepared to both understand other people's viewpoints and to defuse conflicts more readily.

THE NINE ENNEAGRAM TYPES

Type 1: The Reformer/Perfectionist/Idealist

Type 1 individuals are characterised by the rigid principles and pressure they impose on themselves. Their motivation comes from constantly competing with others and with themselves. They like to receive recognition for their efforts and, if they do not receive feedback, will attempt to repress their resulting frustration, which in many cases will eventually be channelled into scathing criticism.

Type 2: The Helper/Altruist/Giver

The attitudes and behaviours associated with this type are dictated by personality traits which are oriented towards others, such as devotion, generosity, supportiveness, willingness to listen, and so on. Type 2 individuals often put the needs of others before their own, although this conceals the fact that their central motivation is a kind of pride: their high self-esteem, which is fuelled by their altruistic actions.

Type 3: The Achiever/Performer/ Motivator

Type 3 individuals are success-oriented and want other people to recognise their achievements, which is the driving force behind their actions. They are pragmatic and enjoy being challenged on a regular basis, and in healthy individuals these qualities make them confident, adaptable people who are always striving to improve themselves. Conversely, unhealthy type 3s may be tempted to resort to lying and scheming to achieve their goals.

Type 4: The Individualist/Romantic/ Artist

Type 4 individuals aspire to be original and distinctive; above all else, they want to stand out from the crowd. They are driven by their desires and their passions, and are the most romantic of all the Enneagram types. They are creative and imaginative, but their inability to control their own emotions can sometimes leave them overwhelmed.

Type 5: The Investigator/Observer/ Thinker

Type 5 individuals prefer to be recognised for their knowledge, their keen observational skills and their knack for finding innovative solutions. When they feel uncomfortable, type 5s tend to withdraw and simply observe the situation, and if left unchecked, this detachment can leave them prone to cynicism or avarice.

Type 6: The Loyalist/Guardian/Sceptic

Type 6 individuals are profoundly honest and never allow themselves to stray from their path, as they are chiefly preoccupied with ensuring their own security. A thriving type 6 will form solid, long-lasting relationships with others, which will in turn give them greater stability and security in their lives. When under pressure, they are besieged by doubts, fears and suspicion. They can become paranoid, and their conversations will start to revolve around their anxieties.

Type 7: The Enthusiast/Epicure/ Adventurer

Type 7 individuals are relentlessly optimistic and upbeat, and find fulfilment in novelty and constantly doing the unexpected. However, if their spontaneity is taken to extremes, their efforts become unfocused and unproductive, and they may neglect their own needs.

Type 8: The Challenger/Protector/Leader

This type is characterised by forceful, combative attitudes. Type 8 individuals are driven by both their instincts and a desire to be in charge, and at their best they are natural, well-respected leaders. However, arrogance can lead them to extremes such as megalomania, vengefulness, or even delusion when reality does not bend to their will.

Type 9: The Peacemaker/Negotiator/ Mediator

The final Enneagram type desires peace and harmony above all, and has a talent for reconciliation. Type 9 individuals are positive, skilled communicators with a zest for life who place great value on social interaction and put other people first, sometimes neglecting their own needs in the process. Their deep-rooted aversion to conflict can lead them to bury their head in the sand, and even to turn to substance abuse in extreme cases.

TO EACH THEIR OWN NEUROSES

Every type has its own strengths and weaknesses. This means that when you discover your type, there is no need to be alarmed if you see it described as "neurotic", "lazy", "delusional", etc. In fact, this is one of the most useful features of the Enneagram: it sheds light on the darker sides of your personality, no matter how unpleasant it can be to acknowledge them. This kind of self-discovery means that we must face our shortcomings so that we can correct them – after all, in the long term, healing is should always be our primary goal. At its core, self-help is about minimising and even eliminating unhealthy behaviour.

Case study: Emily

Emily has discovered that she is a type 2, meaning that her personality is associated with traits such as altruism and helpfulness, but also with pride. This comes as a shock to Emily, as she has never thought of herself as proud. She does not like to think of her actions as being motivated by self-interest, so she refuses to acknowledge it. However, when she digs deeper she realises that pride and caring for others are two sides of the same coin: she longs to get the recognition she feels she deserves for her work and her behaviour, and for her love to be reciprocated. As a result, she has a habit of sometimes altering her own personality to fit in and please others at any cost. Emily reflects on her daily life and suddenly everything becomes clear to her, viewed from this new perspective. Over time, she gradually comes to accept this "neurotic" aspect of her personality which she had previously rejected.

As you can see from the brief descriptions above, each of the types has their own strengths and weaknesses: no one is perfect, and no Enneagram type is better than any other. All of the nine types have the potential for greatness, in their own ways, when they are totally fulfilled and thriving, as well as the potential to fall into unhealthy, self-destructive behaviours.

You should also bear in mind that these categories are not set in stone: our thoughts and behaviours vary depending on the situations we find ourselves in. While brushes with both the positive and the negative personality traits associated with each type are unavoidable, we must therefore make an effort to nourish the positive and cut out the negative.

TOP TIPS

- Approach this process with confidence and with a genuine desire to improve your well-being. In order to do so, it is important not to doubt the process, which has proven its worth, and, above all, not to doubt yourself and your own capacity for self-improvement.
- Stay objective, as this is the only way to ensure that exercises like discovering your Enneagram are effective in practice. Taking a step back and observing yourself objectively is great progress in and of itself.
- Ask your close friends and family to help. The previous tip can be difficult to put into practice, so the most productive approach is often to get those closest to you involved in the process.
- Do not fret over the results. For many people, the initial thrill of discovering their Enneagram type and its positive qualities is soon diminished by an unflattering explanation of their behaviour. This is a key part of the process in the sense that it tends to give the participant

a bit of a shock. Naturally, this pivotal stage of the Enneagram can be discouraging, but this is where the real work begins.

- Take a moment to absorb the results and try to re-evaluate events that happened earlier in your life in the light of this analysis. No process which aims to help you understand yourself better should be rushed; as is often the case, this journey is as enriching as the destination. If you have found the results disconcerting, take the time to mull things over, as this is sure to make it easier for you to engage with the work that follows.
- Think about what "positive growth" could entail for your type and behaviour.
- Learn more about your type and its full description: your base type, your wing, and your directions of integration and disintegration. At this point, you should try to identify any pre-existing tendencies to adopt alternative behaviours as you grow and develop.
- Think about specific ways you could improve your behaviour on a daily basis. Think back on events which occurred in the past and replay them in your head using a different approach which cuts out the compulsive behaviours

associated with your type. This will help you to train yourself to react differently.

- Consider other kinds of self-help therapy so that you can use the Enneagram more effectively and on your own terms.
- Use what you have learned to improve your understanding of other people. One of the greatest assets of the Enneagram is the way it enhances your perception of the wide range of individual motivations that drive different people. This is a chance to grow by becoming more understanding and more tolerant of other people's behaviour.

FAQS

SURELY USING THE ENNEAGRAM TO ANALYSE PEOPLE'S PERSONALITIES IS REALLY ABOUT PUTTING PEOPLE IN BOXES?

On the contrary, the Enneagram aims to free us from our constraints and to help us understand ourselves. Discovering your type means becoming aware of your own thought processes and behavioural tendencies. Each individual's inherent nature, as well as their education and life experiences, shapes their way of behaving, which they may not always be fully aware of. This can sometimes prove restrictive, and over time we generally become more set in our ways and reluctant to change. By using the Enneagram to pinpoint these habits, it is possible to overcome them and to find a path that grants us more freedom.

WILL EXAMINING MY PERSONALITY THROUGH THE LENS OF ENNEAGRAM THEORY REALLY HELP ME TO UNDERSTAND MYSELF MORE FULLY?

Yes. Enneagram analysis will reveal certain truths about you, which can often be surprising.

In fact, each person's strengths and weaknesses can usually be grouped together and linked to fundamental behaviours which are driven by specific motivations. This is known as an Enneagram type, which has many different facets in the form of various personality traits. Once this inherent nature has been brought to light, delving further into Enneagram theory can lead to solutions: each type is also comprised of wings and poles, in addition to the base type.

The wings are the two bases which are adjacent to a person's base type on the enneagram figure, and will also have a certain influence on them, though one wing is usually more dominant than the other. Observing the characteristics of your wings, or even just your dominant wing, is therefore a good first step towards personal growth.

The enneagram figure also contains arrows which connect each type with two others, which represent the personality traits that an individual tends to adopt when they are in a comfortable, healthy situation, or under immense pressure.

> **Case study: Emily (continued)**
> One weakness shared by many type 2 individuals like Emily is a tendency to constantly attempt to conform to the expectations of those around them in order to please them and be loved in return. One way this manifests is Emily's compulsive habit of saying "yes" to everything – even when she does not entirely agree. She now knows that it can be beneficial to adopt the attitude of a type 8 individual and learn to say "no" sometimes.

As you can see, the Enneagram can provide you with a great deal of food for thought regarding yourself and your behaviour, and will enable you to better grasp all the complexities of human personalities.

HOW CAN I APPLY ENNEAGRAM THEORY IN MY PROFESSIONAL LIFE?

There are many situations which can arise in the workplace in which individual personalities play a crucial role. In the following examples we will examine a few of these situations and show how Enneagram theory can be applied to them:

- **Recruitment:** from now on, when your potential future employer inevitably asks you the dreaded question, "What are your greatest strengths and weaknesses?" – often a pivotal moment in the hiring process – you will be able to provide an insightful, measured answer. This will help you to stand out, as you will show the interviewer that you are in control of your own personality and that you can turn each of your strengths and weaknesses to your advantage.
- **Conflict:** no matter whether they arise from misunderstandings or from an unavoidable dispute, disagreements can often cause frustration and problems in the workplace. Although it is essential to know yourself and therefore be able to pinpoint what is bothering you and the reasons why the situation

is making you uncomfortable, this is often totally overlooked in mainstream conflict resolution strategies. The Enneagram reminds us that our own perceptions play a key role in any conflict, and guides us towards an internally-focused approach based on dealing with those perceptions.

- **Teamwork:** knowing and understanding the reasons why someone might be driven to act in a certain way can be an incredibly effective way of optimising team relations. Given that each type is characterised by the way they react to events, an awareness of the different ways each person working on a project processes information can be invaluable.

IS THERE AN IDEAL PROFESSION FOR EACH TYPE?

Absolutely not: the Enneagram should never be about determinism. However, given that Enneagram analysis is based on individual motivations, knowing your type, your dominant wing and your directions of integration and disintegration – and, by extension, the motivations associated with them – can give you a general idea of the roles you might be naturally suited to. But be careful not to use this as the basis for all your choices – this approach is designed to be used as a tool, not as a diktat.

If you are contemplating a particular job, the Enneagram will first and foremost help you to discover which of your personality traits would be beneficial to you in that role, and to help you identify any potential stumbling blocks.

ARE THERE SOME TYPES WHICH ARE FUNDAMENTALLY INCAPABLE OF UNDERSTANDING EACH OTHER?

As mentioned previously, the Enneagram is not about ignoring reality: everyone is different and, as a result, one person's preferred way of doing things, motivations and thought processes may not be identical to someone else's. Knowing how the other person thinks is therefore an essential component of effective collaboration, meaning that the Enneagram can help to ensure that a company or team functions smoothly.

This means that each type is capable of understanding any other – provided that each individual has an idea of how the other person thinks and what motivates them. This knowledge will make negotiations easier and, in general, using the Enneagram in a business setting will help you to gain a better understanding of how other people think. Each type will have certain expectations which reflect their motivations, and when they are stymied it inevitably produces frustration, misunderstandings and conflict.

CAN MY TYPE CHANGE OVER TIME?

In theory, a person's dominant type should remain constant throughout their life, and will always be the type that their personality most closely corresponds to. However, given that everyone's personality will gradually become more complex over time, they may gradually distance themselves from certain traits associated with their base type and take on other characteristics instead. In fact, this is the purpose of the Enneagram: getting to know yourself better so that you can make the most of your strengths and resist giving in to your shortcomings, while also taking on the strengths of the other types when possible.

The approach championed by the Enneagram takes the ways our personalities develop into account through the incorporation of the wings and the directions of integration and disintegration into the theory. These elements complement the base type and help to explain the richness and complexities of human personalities.

OVER TO YOU

We hope that this short introduction to the Enneagram has given you some insight into the usefulness of this technique and the scope of its potential effects. This method is not simply about categorising your personality using the base types, wings and directions of integration and disintegration; it also provides guidance for self-improvement.

> "First of all I would like to endorse that aspect of "working on oneself" which is the acknowledgement of the truth about oneself and one's life in spite of the discomfort or pain that this may involve – in other words, intimate confession. [...] Indeed, the truth about ourselves can free us, for once we have truly understood something about ourselves, it will change without "our" attempt to change it." (Naranjo, 1994: 271-271)

Once you have discovered your type, or at least identified the types that you most closely resemble, the rest is up to you. By simply embarking on this journey of self-discovery, you have already begun the transformation process.

However, you may need to broaden your knowledge and learn about other techniques to help you throughout this journey. Practical methods such as NLP or EFT may also come in useful, and using the Enneagram in combination with these techniques will allow you to unlock its full potential.

- NLP (neuro-linguistic programming) is a thoroughly modern psychotherapy technique which, like the Enneagram, has proven incredibly useful in the workplace. It focuses on how individuals perceive reality in different ways and, by harnessing the relationship between our behaviour and our dominant senses, enables participants to consciously reject their habitual behavioural patterns in favour of an alternative. Given that each Enneagram type corresponds to an aspect of NLP, combining these two methods can only result in an even more profound understanding of the self.
- EFT (Emotional Freedom Techniques) is another path to self-discovery. This method involves tapping on the body's energy meridian points in order to disperse the negative emotions produced by certain events, as

these can cause blockages which prevent us from moving towards improved behavioural wellbeing.

These three techniques share very similar fundamental principles, and they all agree that no one lacks the resources necessary for self-improvement. Using the Enneagram as a starting point, everyone is capable of recognising their own worth and of enriching any social environment they inhabit.

We want to hear from you!
Leave a comment on your online library
and share your favourite books on social media!

FURTHER READING

BIBLIOGRAPHY

- Lapid-Bogda, G. (2007) *L'ennéagramme. Se connaître pour réussir.* Issy-les-Moulineaux: ESF Éditeur.

- Naranjo, C. (1994) *Character and Neurosis: An Integrative View.* Nevada City: Gateways.

- Rognoni, A. (1997) *L'ennéagramme. Nouvelle méthode d'analyse psychologique.* Paris: Éditions de Vecchi.

ADDITIONAL SOURCES

- Riso, D. R. and Hudson, R. (1996) *Personality Types: Using the Enneagram for Self-Discovery.* Revised edition. New York: Houghton Mifflin Harcourt.

- Riso, D. R. and Hudson, R. (2000) *Understanding the Enneagram: The Practical Guide to Personality Types.* Revised edition. New York: Houghton Mifflin Harcourt.

- The Enneagram Institute website: <https://www. enneagraminstitute.com>

50MINUTES.com
History
Business
Coaching
Book Review
Health & Wellbeing
ISHIKAWA DIAGRAM
Anticipate and solve problems within your business
Material Method Machine
Mother Nature Measure Men
THE BATTLE OF AUSTERLITZ
NETWORKING
IMPROVE YOUR GENERAL KNOWLEDGE
IN A BLINK OF AN EYE !
www.50minutes.com